GOOD GRIEF!

Hope, Help, and a little Humor for
your Journey from Wife to Widow

To:

_____

From:

_____

Date:

_____

Message:

_____

_____

_____

"She is clothed with strength and dignity,
and she laughs without fear of the future."
Proverbs 31:25 NLT

GOOD GRIEF!

Hope, Help, and a little Humor for
your Journey from Wife to Widow

n

Jody Noland
with illustrations by Alejo Porras

GOOD GRIEF!

Unless otherwise noted, Scripture taken from the Holy Bible, New International Version ©. Copyright © 1973, 1978, 1984 by International Bible Society. Used by permission of Zondervan. All rights reserved.

Scripture quotations marked (NLT) are taken from the Holy Bible, New Living Translation, copyright © 1996. Used by permission of Tyndale House Publishers, Inc., Wheaton, Illinois 60189. All rights reserved.

Scripture taken from The Message. Copyright ©1993, 1994, 1995, 1996, 2000, 2001, 2002. Used by permission of NavPress Publishing Group.

Printed in the United States of America

ISBN: 978-0-9885769-2-6

To my extraordinary daughter,
Annie, with all my love.

Thank you for being my relentless
champion, loving and hilarious truth-
teller and grace-filled encourager.

I'm so thankful God picked me to
be your momma!

———————————————

*"Your love has given me great joy
and encouragement."*
Philemon 7

CONTENTS

GOOD GRIEF!

Hope, Help, and a little Humor for
your Journey from Wife to Widow

DEAR READER

WHEN MY HUSBAND DIED a decade ago, I was given a number of books by well-meaning friends that were full of solid, scriptural advice. But, oh, were they serious. And, like most widows I know, I put those books on the shelf and never opened them again. Life was heavy enough.

After a recent divorce, my shelves once more filled with books—heavy, undoubtedly useful, tomes I barely opened. It was hard to find much to smile about in those books.

Thankfully, God wired me with a sense of humor. During the most difficult seasons of life, my greatest source of laughter has been my own foibles. Time and time again, I've said: "Well, I can laugh, or I can cry. I choose to laugh." Often, a cartoon rendition of the situation would pop up in my brain and I would laugh as I tried to focus on the more humorous side of things.

My desire in creating *Good Grief!* is to encourage and refresh you. No, there's nothing intrinsically good or amusing about suddenly becoming single. But there are "treasures hidden in the darkness" and countless examples of God's goodness to be found in the midst of the sorrow. You, too, can find reasons to laugh.

I hope and pray this book will bring a smile to your face and that my hard-earned wisdom will be helpful. I especially hope that you won't feel quite so alone and realize there is a sisterhood in these struggles. More than anything, I pray that you will come to know, love, and trust Jesus at a deeper, sweeter level than ever before.

Your fellow overcomer,

Jody

"And I will give you treasures hidden in the darkness -
secret riches. I will do this so you may know that I am the
LORD, the God of Israel, the one who calls you by name."
Isaiah 45:3 NLT

CHAPTER ONE

JODY GROWS UP

"That's not exactly what I'd call a highlight reel"

LET'S FACE IT: being a Jesus follower doesn't mean that life will be simple, easy or trouble-free. Generally, the opposite seems to be true. God often uses suffering from a myriad of sources to shape and refine our character so that we continue to reflect Him more. I love the image of God's light shining through our brokenness. I hope and pray that's the story of my life.

My life before Jesus wasn't pretty. It consisted of worldly success and moral failures. Finally, in my late twenties, I understood the truth that "there is no condemnation in Christ Jesus," (Romans 8:1) and grasped the amazing reality that Jesus died a brutal death on the cross to pay for my sins. I was undone. Asking for His forgiveness and surrendering to Jesus as my Lord and Savior changed my life forever. What a priceless and completely undeserved gift to not only be forgiven and have the promise of eternal life, but for the same Holy Spirit who raised Jesus from the dead to come and live inside of me! (Romans 8:11)

In 2009, I was widowed after nearly twenty-five years of a character-building marriage. My husband had been diagnosed with Stage 4 liver cancer in March of that year and died just a few, brutal months later. At the time of his death, I was in my early fifties. Our daughter was entering her junior year of high school.

One year later, during the fall of my daughter's senior year, my own father was diagnosed with pancreatic cancer and died within a month of his diagnosis. Eight months later, my heartbroken mom passed away. My parents, who lived 700 miles away, had been married for sixty-eight years at the time of my dad's death. I was balancing life as a newly single parent with the joys and busyness of my daughter's senior year, along with supporting my airplane-flight-away, elderly parents in their last days. It felt like I was being squished between the unyielding doors of the Atlanta airport's Plane-Train. (If you've ever made the mistake of trying to keep those doors open, you know exactly what I mean.)

Fortunately, I was with my parents and my husband at the end of their lives. Before my husband's passing, the closest I had been to death was scurrying past the door of the hospital's morgue as a terrified, teenaged candy striper. But God used those three experiences of walking with family "through the valley of the shadow of death" to help me appreciate the sacred and bittersweet time when a loved one is approaching the end of their earthly journey. Not everyone has the chance to say goodbye. I'm so grateful I did.

Just two short months after my mom's death, my only child left for college. Life seemed surreal. Over a two-year time period, every major role in my life ended. Yes, I was still a mom, but the day-to-day responsibilities shifted dramatically once my daughter left for college.

With my newly emptied nest, I felt as though I was finding my way through a maze, blindfolded. I kept asking God *"Now what?"* I was scared and uncertain, but I kept trying to do the next right thing in front of me.

Baby step by baby step, I began to refine and share a dream that had been germinating for a long time. The seeds of inspiration for *Leave Nothing Unsaid* (www.LeaveNothingUnsaid.com) had been planted many years before, but my personal experiences with loss dramatically increased my passion for its importance and relevance. I was fortunate enough to gain substantial traction with my message and receive some incredible media coverage.

In 2015, I finally summoned my courage to date again.

With prodding from trusted friends, I decided to try an online dating site. After weeding through many "no thanks," (what is it with sixty-year-old men posing bare-chested in front of their Harleys?) I met a widower who seemed to be Prince Charming. After a romance-filled courtship, we married in 2017. Before our first wedding anniversary, the seeming fairy tale quickly became a nightmare when I discovered my new husband hadn't meant the "forsaking all others" part of our marriage covenant. His unfaithfulness shattered my heart. We tried reconciling for a few months, but it quickly became apparent that his character was not changing. So, I proceeded with divorce. Less than eighteen months after remarrying with great hope and anticipation, I found myself picking up the pieces of my life, wondering how I could have made such a colossal mistake.

I've finally stopped asking "why, God?" and instead ask "what, God?" and "how, God?"

Over the course of a decade, I've experienced the death of my spouse and both of my parents. I've weathered wave upon wave of grief and faced the loneliness that comes with an empty nest. I've fallen in love again and had my heart shattered in a million pieces. And I've pursued a dream with lots of starts and stops along the way. I've been through a LOT. Yet through it all, and truly by the grace of God, I have survived, revived, and even begun to thrive!

I've finally stopped asking "why, God?" and instead ask "what, God?" and "how, God?"

5

"What do you want me to learn from this?"

"How can I use this experience to help others?"

I believe, with all my heart, that *God wastes nothing*. Even in my darkest hours, I've been able to find humorous moments. I've been supported by the love and prayers of wonderful family and friends. I've experienced God's faithfulness and learned He really does bring beauty from ashes.

Wife. Mother. Daughter. Widow. Orphan. Girl Friend. Fiancée. Bride. Divorcée. Friend. Speaker. Writer. Over the last decade, those labels have described me. And, at times, I've allowed those labels to define me. But none of those really ARE me. They describe my life circumstances. I have come to believe that I am: A Child of God. Beloved. Cherished. Chosen. This is my true identity, and it's your true identity, too, no matter what this life may throw your way.

"Praise be to the God and Father of our Lord Jesus Christ, the Father of compassion and the God of all comfort, who comforts us in all our troubles, so that we can comfort those in any trouble with the comfort we ourselves receive from God."
2 Corinthians 1:3-4

CHAPTER TWO

THE GIFT OF A LONG GOOD BYE

*"I'll have to go soon.
Thanks for waiting with me."*

A GIFT? SURELY, I JEST. How could a terminal diagnosis for a loved one be considered a gift?

A long goodbye is a gift because it affords both of you the opportunity to have closure. To express the depths of your love and gratitude for one another. To ask painful but necessary questions.

Talk to anyone whose spouse has died suddenly. I guarantee they have regrets about things they wish they had said or asked. It's inevitable. Although we might proclaim that we want to "live every day like it's our last," the reality is, most people don't. Quite frankly, it's impossible.

When someone has a terminal illness, you know the end is approaching but you don't know when it will happen. If hospice care has been recommended, the end is likely coming very soon.

My hospice experiences with three family members were all different yet had commonalities—the unknown timeline of how the illness would progress, and the ever-present love and compassion of the hospice workers. You will never know the exact number of days ahead of you, how long your loved one will be conscious or coherent, or exactly what their symptoms will be. It is natural to be fearful because of all the uncertainty.

Please do everything you can to eulogize the living. Put your feelings in writing (perhaps in letter form) and tell your spouse what they mean to you, expressing how much you love them and why. Affirm the character qualities you cherish. Recount your favorite happy memories. Read that letter to them over and over again, even if they lose consciousness near the end of their days. (See www.LeaveNothingUnsaid. com if you need help with letter writing.)

Writing a letter at this stage might seem odd or ill-timed, but the benefit of writing about those feelings in the moment is that you can continue to read the letter aloud, even when you feel emotionally depleted and the journey becomes more difficult. At some point, you won't have the energy to think creatively or search for the perfect words. But you will be able to read something meaningful and heartfelt that you've already composed.

Another idea is to take a picture of your two hands together, yours holding theirs. Yes, this, too, might seem odd, but the photograph will become very meaningful to you in the future. Those hands have communicated love, strength and encouragement to one another over the years, and having a picture of your two hands together will be a tender reminder of that mutual support.

Please do everything you can to eulogize the living.

Encourage other family members and close friends to write notes and letters, too. Far better to tell your loved one what they mean to you while they are still living than to wait and express those sentiments at their funeral. Consider placing the notes in a basket near their bedside so that they can be read and re-read or tape the notes up in a visible place (around a doorframe) where they can be seen.

If possible, encourage your spouse to write letters to your children. Even short letters affirming a few special character qualities and expressing love, hope and prayers for the future will be cherished by the recipients in the days and years to come. Short, recorded messages will also become priceless treasures for the recipients. Not everyone approaching death can or will want to do this, even when offered assistance. If you receive resistance, let it go.

Ask the necessary questions. Make sure you know about finances, legal documents, trusted advisors, accounts, passwords, and insurance policies. Get a notebook and write the answers down in one place. Find out your loved one's wishes for funeral arrangements. Soon, you will be responsible for all aspects of this new life, so think through the things you will need to know now. As difficult as it is to have these discussions, please don't wait. A hospice patient's condition can change very quickly from day to day.

At some point near the end of their life, your loved one might become unconscious or heavily sedated to control pain. Even then, assume they can still hear you. Keep talking, keep playing uplifting music, keep reading Scripture about Heaven, and keep telling them what they mean to you.

Make use of the wonderful online resource of Caring Bridge (www.caringbridge.org) to share updates and prayer requests with those who are concerned. Not only will you be spared from endlessly repeating status reports, you will receive encouragement from the kind sentiments left by friends.

It's a time of waiting and wondering. Cry out to God like never before. Keep praying. Repeat meaningful verses of Scripture over and over again. Keep saying "I trust you, Jesus." Don't lose heart.

While you are sitting and waiting with your loved one, you might feel as though you are at a train station and the train bound for Glory is coming soon. You can hear the train in the distance, but don't know its exact arrival time.

When they finally climb aboard and draw their last breath on Earth, you will be so grateful for the sacred honor of being by their side and of seeing them off as they transition to Eternity.

"All the days ordained for me were written in your book before one of them came to be."
Psalm 139:16

CHAPTER THREE

CAREGIVER, A CODEWORD FOR "EXHAUSTED"

"I'm... fine... I'm fine."

IF YOU'RE A CAREGIVER, you're undoubtedly exhausted. It goes with the territory. Mental, physical and, likely, spiritual exhaustion. Bone-weary exhaustion.

As a result of your loved one's declining condition, more and more of the burden of living has fallen on you. The stress and uncertainty that accompanies a terminal diagnosis for your loved one puts tremendous, non-stop pressure on you. You are grieving for everyone concerned: your spouse, yourself, your children and grandchildren, friends, and other family.

You want to fix it but are completely helpless. You've tried everything. Your heart (and your back) is breaking.

You might fear the unknown future as the disease continues to progress. Perhaps you've never been around death before. You worry that your loved one's pain will become uncontrollable, their mental acuity might be slipping, and that adds another layer of torment for you.

Does the doctor seem to be sugar-coating reality by avoiding your questions? The truth is that medicine is often more of an art than a science. Hospice workers will often say that it could be days, weeks, or even months. Only the Lord really knows the number of our days. And that uncertainty is hard and frustrating, especially for the caregiver.

Don't be surprised if you find yourself telling God that you can't go on much longer. He understands and offers His strength to sustain you. You might find yourself begging God to take your loved one to Heaven. That's a completely normal response, especially with the burden you are carrying. Don't think you're a bad person if you have those feelings. But once your loved one is gone, you'll find yourself wishing for one more hug, one more hand squeeze, one more smile. As long as God keeps your loved one on this earth, try to savor the moments together.

Friends offer to help but you really don't know what to ask them to do. Time and time again, you'll hear "you've got to take care of yourself," but that seems selfish and impossible right now.

A wise friend repeatedly told me "you can't pour from an empty pitcher." I nodded my head in agreement but didn't really know how to heed her advice. I ended up being unable to sleep through the night for many months and became completely worn down and worn out. Miraculously, I didn't develop any serious illnesses.

Find the discipline and courage to take care of yourself.

Find the discipline and courage to take care of yourself. Carve out a few minutes every daily for renewal. If someone offers to come and stay with your loved one, say yes. When friends ask what they can do to help, ask them to visit and give you the gift of some time. Even if you don't leave the house, you can go and take a nap somewhat peacefully, knowing that someone else is temporarily in charge.

If possible, take a walk in a beautiful environment, enjoy an uninterrupted cup of coffee, journal, read your Bible, listen to uplifting music, go to a movie, get a massage, have lunch with a friend or do something else that is renewing to you. You're not being selfish. You're being a good steward of your own body and mind. And you will be better equipped to continue to love and serve others, most importantly, your courageous loved one.

"Teach us to number our days,
that we may gain a heart of wisdom."
Psalm 90:12

CHAPTER FOUR

THIS MUST BE A BAD DREAM
(a.k.a. Funeral Planning)

*"...and these are our exquisite waterfall plots.
They are ONLY $20.000."*

I KNOW, I KNOW... it seems like you are in the middle of a bad dream. Sadly, you are not. You need to plan a funeral and all that goes with it.

Your loved one might be in the late stages of an illness or you might be reeling from the shock of an unexpected death. Either way, planning a funeral is the task at hand. And it's the pits.

As unconscionable as it might seem, there are some opportunistic people out there who will prey on your vulnerability and encourage you to spend money unnecessarily. Be aware and be wise! While getting the best of everything might seem an appropriate way to express your devotion, your loved one won't care once they are gone! And you will spend thousands of dollars more than necessary.

Here are a few things to consider:

• **CREMATION OR BURIAL?** If possible, ask your loved one in advance for their preference. It's not a pleasant question or discussion, but their wishes should be honored.

My husband wanted to be buried at a nearby cemetery, but we never purchased plots. While family was visiting, and I could take time away from my husband's care, I gulped back my emotions and headed to the cemetery to inquire about buying two plots. A smiling, overly solicitous salesman invited me to join him in a golf cart and commenced a tour of the expansive cemetery. First stop: the lakeside plots. Those were only $25,000 each. After the next stop, the waterfall plots, (a "bargain" at only $20,000 each), I suggested to the smarmy salesman that we start at the bottom of their price range and work our way up as we looked at available options.

He grimaced, sighed, and then took me to what I dubbed the "Billy Goat Section." Those plots were located at the very back of the cemetery on the side of a hill next to a chain link fence. Definitely not optimal. I could just picture an interment service there, and Heaven help us if it rained! All I could imagine was a mudslide washing my husband's casket and all the mourners down the steep hill.

After reviewing their depressing range of options, we drove back to the office. On the way, I asked about the cost of grave markers and nearly choked at his multi-thousand-dollar reply. He wasn't amused when I asked if a stake and a Sharpie would suffice.

As we were driving by the oldest and most beautiful part of the cemetery, I inquired about plot availability in that section. "*Sorry, those are sold out.*" Then, I posed the million-dollar question: "*Do people ever resell their plots?*" His answer said it all: "*We can't.*" My next question was "*How do people do it? An online site like Craigslist?*" He told me that was the most common way.

As soon as I arrived home, I began to search online. Lo and behold, I found *two* plots in the most desirable section of that same cemetery being offered for less than the cost of *one* plot offered in their Billy Goat Section. I contacted the seller and quickly made arrangements to purchase those two plots. (**Disclaimer:** There are a lot of horror stories about buying things from online sites like Craigslist. Please proceed with caution. Take a trusted friend or relative with you to evaluate and especially when exchanging funds.)

Cremation is much less costly, but it's not for everyone. It reduces the number of decisions that must be made and gives the bereaved family more flexibility with the timing and planning of a memorial service. There is always the question of "What do I do with the ashes?" but many options exist. Cemeteries typically have a columbarium where ashes can be placed; ashes can be scattered at a special location on a later date or kept in a container in one's home.

My parents chose to be cremated and, at first, I was shocked at their decision (honestly, more than a little uncomfortable.) But I understood and respected their wishes and found the process less complicated and far less expensive. Yes, there were a few horrifying moments, such as when the undertaker asked if "I wanted to put 'Mom' in the trunk of the car or in the front seat with me?" Or when I struggled with whether I should bring their remains into my hotel room the night before their interment services. (I brought them into my hotel room. What if the rental car was stolen overnight?) I pushed through those difficult moments and imagined more mental cartoon images. Yes, I even had to laugh at how often life seems stranger than fiction.

An abundance of information about cremation exists on the Internet. Understanding the pros, cons, and costs of the various alternatives is helpful, but ultimately, it is a very personal and individual decision.

• **EMBALMING.** From my perspective, when a loved one is deceased, I don't understand why you would do something artificial to delay the natural process.

• **CASKET AND GRAVE MARKER.** When I realized how much money could be saved by looking for alternate sources, I decided to search online for caskets and grave markers. I learned that I could save a significant amount by buying the casket and grave marker from online suppliers. The products offered were the same options available from the funeral home and cemetery, but for much less money. The delivery of the casket was extremely prompt. Recent legislative changes have provided alternative sources which offer savings and protection for the consumer.

• **OTHER FUNERAL EXPENSES.** Even when saving money on the most expensive parts of a funeral, the costs can quickly add up. Expenses can include flowers, musicians, visitation costs, food, honorarium for ministers, church or funeral home expenses, to name a few. Whenever possible, simplify, simplify, simplify. Remember that your love is not measured by how much you spend on your loved one's funeral.

Remember that your love is not measured by how much you spend on your loved one's funeral.

Some costs can't be avoided or alternatively sourced. I was stunned at the cost to transport my husband's body to the funeral home— $850 for less than a two-mile drive! The drivers didn't seem to be amused when I asked if they could drive my deceased husband around the Atlanta Perimeter to get our money's worth.

• **BE PREPARED.** A friend whose husband had recently died at home under hospice care gave me an invaluable piece of advice as I prepared for my own husband's death. She said: "Don't watch as they remove his body from your house. It's a memory you will never forget." Amidst the shocking reality of his passing, I would not have thought of that, but was so grateful to have been forewarned.

As painful as it is, think about what you will wear for the funeral. Do you need a friend to loan you an appropriate black dress? Start gathering your favorite pictures of your husband and put them in frames to display at the visitation or in the church foyer before the service. If your loved one is alert and willing, ask them to help write their own obituary and provide preferences for the speakers and music for their memorial service.

• **ACCEPT HELP.** Friends might offer to help. **Let them.** You will be in a daze and the more support you have, the better. Whether it is planning and providing a meal for guests after the funeral service, housing out-of-town company, picking people up at the airport, setting up and taking down photographs for the visitation and funeral, cleaning your house, or stocking your refrigerator, learn to say *"yes, thank you."* Many people really do want to help, and they often don't know what to say or do. Be a grateful recipient of all the help that is offered. Keep a list of the kind things people are doing in a notebook. You'll have plenty of time later to write thank-you notes.

God seems to provide special grace and comfort during the time of a funeral. When you look back, you'll realize you were in a mental and emotional fog. Most of us experience that feeling. But that, too, seems to be God's grace. The details will come together. Try to relax. Savor the love of family and friends. Celebrate your loved one's life and take some deep breaths. A challenging new chapter of life is about to begin.

• **WHAT ABOUT YOUR OWN PLANS?** When you are single, for whatever reason, does this apply to you? One of the most loving and unselfish things you can do for your family is to plan ahead. Do as much of your own advance planning as possible. Draft your obituary. Make sure you have an updated will and medical directives in place with clear instructions about the location of the original copies. Prepay for funeral services or set aside money to cover those costs. Purchase a funeral plot or space in a columbarium. Select the music, speakers, and scriptures for your own memorial service. Put all pertinent information in a clearly marked file or box in your home and tell a responsible loved one or friend. When the time comes, your family will be exceedingly grateful for your thoughtfulness.

"Do not let your hearts be troubled. You believe in God; believe also in me. My Father's house has many rooms; if that were not so, would I have told you that I am going there to prepare a place for you? And if I go and prepare a place for you, I will come back and take you to be with me that you also may be where I am."

John 14:1-3

CHAPTER FIVE

"NEW NORMAL"

"Coffee?"

AFTER THE FUNERAL, when family and out-of-town guests have departed and everyone has returned to their regular routines, you'll find yourself in a place you never expected, an often-lonely island called "New Normal."

The best way I can describe my introduction to the world of New Normal was having an overwhelming sense that the oxygen had been sucked out of the room. Gone were all of the supportive family and friends. My daughter was back at school. And I was eerily aware of the complete quiet. I felt numb, exhausted and in a complete brain fog. The reality that life would never be the same again hit full force.

If you've been through loss and major life change, I can almost guarantee that you've had someone superciliously say, "Better get used to it. This is your 'New Normal.'" And if you're like me, you've probably wanted to slug them. So often, those words come from someone whose "normal" is rocking along in life as usual. No white caps on their waves. Occasional bobbing, but that's about it.

Your "new normal" is not something you ever saw coming. While you're well aware that every person's life has an eventual end date, you always thought that date would be later rather than sooner for the ones you love. Wouldn't you like to stand on a rooftop and scream: *"I never asked for this. I don't want a 'new normal'!!! Where are you, God? Why me?"*

Don't be surprised if in the early days of this new season you find yourself doing scatter-brained things. After never locking myself out of my house for thirty years, I did it three times in the same week! Although I have a black belt in self-deprecation, I encourage you not *Written lists will be your friend, even for the simplest things.* to beat yourself up for innocent mistakes. You are exhausted and in shock. Written lists will be your friend, even for the simplest things.

Feeling overwhelmed and frozen is completely normal. Slowly but surely, things will get better. Try to just take life a day at a time. And if a day seems too overwhelming, take an hour at a time. Your resilience will build. The truth that "His grace is sufficient; His power is made perfect in our weakness" (2 Corinthians 2:9) is a reality you will experience firsthand. But it's something that you will likely see in hindsight. You probably won't hop out of bed each morning saying "Oh, what a beautiful morning. Wow, do I feel God's strength today." Instead, you will muster the energy and ability to press through the challenges of each day, one moment at a time.

Don't put pressure on yourself with timeframes. Yes, you have thank you notes to write. Yes, you need to clear out your spouse's clothes. Yes, you need to figure out which end is up regarding financial planning. But it doesn't all need to happen tomorrow. Take it slowly. Don't make big changes quickly. Give yourself grace. You'd give it to anyone else. Now, give it to yourself.

Trust God with each new day. You'll make it. I promise.

"Don't worry about anything;
instead, pray about everything.
Tell God what you need, and thank Him for all He has done.
Then you will experience God's peace, which exceeds
anything we can understand. His peace will guard your
hearts and minds as you live in Christ Jesus."
Philippians 4:6-7 NLT

CHAPTER SIX

THEY SAID WHAT?

"I'm so sorry, I know how hard it is...
I still miss Mr. Whiskers so much!"

BRACE YOURSELF. You won't believe the things well-meaning people will say.

Whether you are dealing with the heartbreak of your loved one's terminal diagnosis or their tragic death, you will hear some doozies. Count on it.

If you're not careful, those insensitive comments can take root and start to build bitterness and resentment in your heart and eventually isolate you. Please don't let that happen.

My best advice: Just try to smile sweetly, say thank you, and press on. If a comment is particularly offensive, kindly tell the source that you know they mean well but that their comment is not helpful. (You might keep a list of the worst things that people have said to you and have a good laugh about it at a later point. Or, get a punching bag to take out your frustrations.)

Here are a few of my personal favorites:

- *"I know just how you feel. My cat just died."*
- *"Well, at least they lived a good, long life."*
- *"Heaven must have needed another angel."*
- *"There must be unconfessed sin in your life or theirs for this to have happened."*
- *"You must be mad at God."*
- *"You must not have prayed hard enough."*
- *"I had a terrible summer too. Our lake house was being renovated."*
- *"You'll get over it."*
- *"I'm sure God will bring someone else into your life."*
- *"There are worse things than being single."*
- *"Call me if I can do anything for you."*
- Silence. Some people will say nothing at all, as though your life is unchanged. That might be even more hurtful to you since everything has changed.

What **should** people say? Perhaps you too have wondered about the right words to say when comforting someone who is grieving.

These expressions are *generally* well received:

- *"There are no words."*
- *"I am so sorry."*
- *"I'm so sorry for your loss and pain."*
- *"I can't take away the pain, but I am here with you and for you."*
- *"I am going to do XYZ for you."* (Offer something, then, keep your word.)
- A hug without any accompanying words communicates volumes.

Please be forgiving of the people who say insensitive things. The majority mean well but feel very inadequate in knowing what to say to someone who is grieving. The death of a spouse or loved one makes most people feel extremely uncomfortable and is a frightening reminder that they too, could be in your shoes someday. Try to give them grace and learn from their mistakes.

"A word aptly spoken is like apples of gold
in settings of silver."
Proverbs 25:11

CHAPTER SEVEN

THE DREADED "F" WORD

"He made it look so easy..."

EVERY MARRIAGE IS DIFFERENT. The roles and responsibilities vary with every couple, and some wives are well-versed in all things financial and legal. Many, however, are completely clueless.

For women who are unfamiliar with the financial and legal necessities of life, nothing feels quite so overwhelming and terrifying when becoming suddenly single. Unscrupulous people abound, ready to pounce on vulnerable women. Added to that reality is the fear that plagues most women, no matter how sizable her assets—the deep-seated fear of becoming a "bag lady" in later life.

Here are a few suggestions if this is uncharted territory:

• Make sure you have a financial advisor you really trust. Like flies to sugar, persuasive financial providers will start swarming, especially if you are a new widow. Get recommendations from friends. You need someone who is a good match for your personality, who is patient, respectful, wise, willing to answer your questions, and who has a proven track record of success. That might or might not be the same advisor your husband trusted. But it is now your decision, and this relationship is vitally important for your future well-being.

• Consult with your attorney to understand what steps need to be taken to probate a will if your husband has died.

• Ask your accountant about the necessity and timing of filing an estate tax return.

• If your husband has died, be sure to get an adequate number of Death Certificates. You'll need more than a few. I recommend at least ten.

• Make an appointment with Social Security. You may be entitled to Social Security benefits based on your spouse's earnings depending on the length of your marriage. There is also a small, one-time death benefit provided to assist with funeral expenses.

• Update your own legal documents, including your Will, Financial Power of Attorney, and Advance Directives. In case you become medically or mentally incapacitated, you want to ensure that someone you trust is in charge of your well-being and that your assets will be distributed according to your desires in the event of your death.

• Do you have a life insurance policy? If so, be sure to update the beneficiaries if necessary.

• Learn how to do online banking. You will save an incredible amount of time in monthly bill paying after the original set-up. Even if you are feeling overwhelmed, it's important to keep paying your bills on time.

• Monitor your spending and establish a budget. It might take a few iterations to develop a workable budget, but now is the time to learn how to manage your income and expenses. Financial Peace University is offered by many churches and is a great way to learn Biblical truth about managing your money.

• If your spouse left you with financial resources, resist the temptation to make extravagant purchases as a way of numbing your pain.

• Most churches have benevolence funds to assist those who are in financial need. If you are struggling financially, talk to your pastor and ask for help. In addition to assisting you with short-term living expenses, your church may have a member who has financial expertise and would be willing to help you develop a workable financial plan for the future.

• Consider freezing your credit with the three credit bureaus. (Equifax, Experian and TransUnion) If you need to apply for a loan, you can contact the credit bureaus and have the freeze lifted on a temporary basis. This is one way to protect against identity theft and ensure that no one is taking out credit in your name.

• Think about what you will do if you need extended care as you age. The costs of long-term care are prohibitively expensive. Make sure you have a plan in place to provide for yourself if that need arises. "My kids will take care of me" sounds like a great fallback plan but should not be Plan A. If you have a Long-Term Care Insurance policy, do not cancel it! Yes, the premiums might be expensive, but those premiums are far cheaper than the exorbitant cost of long-term care which can quickly deplete your assets. Hybrid products also exist today which combine life insurance with long term care benefits. Ask your financial advisor.

• Plan for your own funeral. For the sake of your children or heirs, having a folder containing the needed information is a wonderfully loving gift. Place all pertinent information in one file and be sure to tell a responsible child or trusted friend the location of that information.

Yes, there is a lot to learn. However, slowly but surely, you can step into these shoes. Gaining financial knowledge and confidence is empowering. Love yourself and your family well by being financially wise. You can do this!

---

*"And my God will meet all your needs according to
the riches of his glory in Christ Jesus."
Philippians 4:19*

CHAPTER EIGHT

SURVIVING THE "FIRSTS"

"I'd better buckle up."

UNDOUBTEDLY, YOU'VE HEARD ABOUT how hard this is—the year of all the "firsts" without your loved one.

The arrival of holidays, birthdays, anniversaries, and other special days is very difficult. I won't sugarcoat it, but you can and will get through them.

Prepare for an onslaught of memories and a flood of emotions on those special days. Try not to be alone, if possible. Whether it's the distraction of going to a movie with a friend or just sitting and having a good cry with someone you trust, lean on your friends and family. Someone who has walked the journey of loss themselves will be especially sensitive to the challenges of the first days.

Sometimes, we think that doing something totally different on important days will help. It doesn't always. Christmas was my husband's favorite holiday, so for the first December after his death, my daughter and I thought it would be a good diversion to celebrate somewhere other than home. As we stared at each other in a hotel room in New York City on Christmas Eve, unable to even find a church holding a Candlelight Service, we thought, *"What have we done?"* We concluded that, for us, it would have been better to be in our familiar and festively decorated home reminiscing about Christmases past than in an unfamiliar setting which made the change in our lives even more stark. Lesson learned.

Consider celebrating your loved one's birthday with your children, family, or close friends. Enjoy their favorite meal or go to their favorite restaurant. You will keep their memory alive by reflecting on their character and the impact they made on your lives. Expressing the things that you miss most about them will be therapeutic for everyone. Share funny stories and look at pictures and home movies. It's healthy to laugh amidst your tears and to be honest about who they were in totality, warts and all.

Reflect, with gratitude, on the happy times you had together over the years. Journal about them. List the things you have lost. Remember the more challenging times, too. It's easy to idealize someone once they are deceased but doing that does not contribute to your healing. Thank God for the gift of time you had together as imperfect people.

Thank God for the gift of time you had together as imperfect people. When you finally survive all of the firsts, and breathe a deep sigh of relief, you'll realize that there really isn't anything magical about the passage of 365 days. Yes, the one-year anniversary of their death will undoubtedly be emotional and the memories vivid. As you think about your loved one, also think of how proud they would be of your strength and courage over the past year. Was it easy? No. Did you do everything perfectly? Probably not. But you made it!

"For I can do everything through Christ
who gives me strength."
Philippians 4:13

CHAPTER NINE

THE TANGLED MESS CALLED EMOTIONS

HAVE YOU EVER HAD several necklaces get tangled? What initially appears to be a simple problem can quickly turn into a knotted mess. And the more you hurry to get things untangled, the more unyielding the knots seem to be.

As we journey through the painful learning process of becoming suddenly single, our lives often feel like that tangled mess. Unexpected and unwanted emotions constantly rise. You experience the searing pain of loss along with guilt, shame, anger, regret, loneliness, fear, self-pity, uncertainty, and hopelessness (often concurrently!) Trying to sort out those emotions can be so difficult. You think you've pushed through a particularly difficult emotion, you'll be hit with an unexpected, tsunami-sized wave of yet another emotion.

Physical symptoms, such as a loss of appetite or energy and insomnia often accompany grief, as does an inability to concentrate or think clearly.

How often have you wondered: *"Am I crazy?"*

Know this, friend: *there's nothing wrong with you.* When you've lost your life partner and your world is turned upside down, it's natural to feel like a jumbled mess. You're not alone and you're not crazy. There is no right way to grieve or correct amount of time. Grief is different for every person. We cycle through the different stages*, often multiple times. What's most important is to not get stuck in a particular stage but to keep pressing forward and dealing with the emotions.

When you've lost your life partner and your world is turned upside down, it's natural to feel like a jumbled mess.

I wish there was a magic button to push that would resolve all of this but there's not. Here are a few tried and true suggestions for regaining emotional stability:

- **EMBRACE YOUR GRIEF.** Healing begins with acknowledging your grief and what you have lost.

* According to Elisabeth Kubler Ross and David Kessler, the five stages of grief are: denial, anger, bargaining, depression, and acceptance.

- **FRIENDS/SAFE PEOPLE.** The pain of grief is flushed out in relationships. You can't do this alone. Yes, the temptation is often to isolate oneself, but please don't. Spend time with a few empathetic friends who won't try to fix you. Allow yourself to cry and express your feelings.

- **JOURNAL.** Write what you are feeling. Sometimes, just the process of getting emotions on paper brings clarity or freedom from that emotion's control of your heart. You don't have to write long entries— express what is in your head and on your heart. Keep writing on a regular basis.

- **GRIEF COUNSELING.** There is never a better time to have someone help you process your feelings and make sure you are headed in the right direction. As you adjust to your new life circumstances, you will continue to have experiences and discoveries that will challenge you. Meeting with a trusted counselor on a regular basis as you go through these adjustments will provide a very welcomed and regular dose of sanity. Ask friends for recommendations.

- **PROCESS HIGHLY TRAUMATIC EXPERIENCES.** An innovative new therapy called E.M.D.R. (Eye Movement Desensitization Reprocessing) is very effective in treating emotional trauma and PTSD. Ask your counselor for a referral to someone who specializes in this treatment.

- **GRIEF SUPPORT GROUPS OR THE GRIEFSHARE PROGRAM.** You won't feel so isolated as you learn about the struggles common to women facing widowhood. You will find wisdom, encouragement, and fellowship in these groups. Most are offered through churches in your community.

- **CONSIDER MEDICAL SUPPORT, IF RECOMMENDED.** Many will immediately dismiss the idea of taking anti-depressants as a sign of weakness or fear the possible development of a dependency on medication. If your doctor or counselor makes this recommendation, please listen. Losing a spouse is incredibly traumatic. It's not a sign of weakness to have prescribed pharmaceutical help for a season of time to regain emotional stability.

- **TAKE STOCK OF THE VOICES IN YOUR HEAD.** What are you believing about yourself? What are you believing about God? Do your feelings square with Scripture? It is so easy to be confused when going through deep loss or drastic change and to unconsciously accept lies. Ask a trusted friend or spiritual mentor to assess your words or actions. Give them permission to be completely honest and provide accountability during this transitional time.

It's so easy to be confused when going through deep loss or drastic change and to unconsciously accept lies.

- **ALLOW YOURSELF TO BE ANGRY.**

You have to let your anger out before you can get over it. Some of us need permission to get angry no matter how justified. Sometimes, we might even feel angry at a deceased spouse for leaving us, even if their death was due to illness or accident. That, too, is a normal, gut-level reaction. A counselor can help you validate those losses.

- **BE FORGIVING: FORGIVE YOURSELF.** Forgive your former spouse, even if they have hurt you deeply. Sometimes painful truths are revealed after a spouse's death, and that requires a whole new level of grace. With deep hurt, forgiveness is generally not a one-step process. (That's why Jesus said to forgive seventy times seven!) Forgive friends and family members who have disappointed you through this journey. As heretical as this might sound, sometimes we need to forgive God for allowing our spouse to die. Forgiveness ultimately benefits you and is an act of obedience to the Lord.

- **WRITE, READ, DESTROY.** One of the most effective ways I've found to process tangled emotions is to write a letter to your deceased spouse. In this letter, I would include: "Things I miss about you. Things I don't miss about you. Things I'm grateful for. Things I wish we had done. Things I forgive you for. Things I need to be forgiven for." Once you've written the letter, read it out loud, perhaps in a location that is meaningful to you. Then, burn it or shred it. This is for your healing, not for anyone else's eyes or ears.

- **ESTABLISH NEW ROUTINES.** When your spouse dies, the structure of your life immediately changes. Responsibilities and routines that might have been in place for decades are suddenly disrupted. Over time, you need to establish new routines and structure. Those are the scaffolds of your life. Determine the daily habits necessary to ensure you are on the right trajectory to finish well.

- **BE PATIENT WITH YOURSELF.** Healing takes time. You probably won't realize that you are making baby steps of progress and getting stronger, day by day, but you are. God promises to bind up the brokenhearted and that includes you!

"He heals the brokenhearted and binds up their wounds."

Psalm 147:3

CHAPTER TEN

PLEASE, DON'T WEED-EAT THE POISON IVY!

"Yard work? Easy peasy!"

PLEASE, PLEASE DON'T USE a Weed Eater on poison ivy. How do I know? Yes, another of my many hard-earned lessons. The result of my brilliant move? My body, having been extensively sprayed with shredded poison ivy, was quickly covered in a horrible rash from head to toe. It was so extreme, and I was so miserable, that I needed a cortisone shot in my derrière to recover!

You see, I tried to bravely step into my new responsibilities of home and yard maintenance. My constant, confidence-building mantra as a new widow was "I can do this!" Yet I was clueless about the basics of operating a Weed Eater and which plants to avoid.

Shortly after the poison ivy debacle, I realized that some things were better left handled by others. I hired a lawn maintenance service. Lesson learned, very painfully.

One of the wisest things I did after my husband's death was to schedule a home inspection. We lived in our home for many years, yet I was accustomed to my husband handling our home repairs—he could fix almost anything. I didn't have the slightest clue about the systems in the house or their required maintenance. The report was enlightening. (And horrifying!) I learned of some significant safety concerns due to items in disrepair. Several unsettling fire risks. The most alarming finding was that our screened porch and deck were not properly attached to the house and could have collapsed under the weight of a small group of people.

After recovering from the shock of the inspection report, the next challenge was to find a trustworthy repairman to address the issues. I met with a number of contractors whom I had found on home improvement sites. Talk about feeling vulnerable! I didn't know who I could trust or whether their estimates and scope of work were realistic or fair. Thankfully, a friend provided a recommendation for an exceptional contractor who exceeded my greatest expectations.

If you find yourself in a similar situation, please ask friends for referrals of reliable contractors who have actually done work for them. There are a lot of shysters out there just waiting to prey on the naive and vulnerable. Don't let that be you! If possible, avoid even mentioning that you are newly widowed. I made the mistake of revealing that to a tree company, and their estimate to remove a tree was twice the other two estimates I received. Coincidence? Maybe, but doubtful. Ask God to protect you and lead you to workmen who are trustworthy and competent.

One of the hardest challenges for many who are newly single is to ask for and accept help from friends. I was fortunate to have several friends who offered to do minor home repairs for me. At first, it was very difficult to say "yes." But I was reminded of the joy I felt being able to help others and decided it was time to humble myself and accept help. I'm so grateful to have experienced God's love and provision through the kindness and generosity of my friends.

What about moving? Your surroundings are a constant reminder of how different life is once you're newly single. And those surroundings impact every woman differently. For most of us, our nest matters a LOT. Only you can determine the best place, long-term, for your healing, and only you know the best financial decision to make for your future.

For some, familiar surroundings provide great comfort. Your home holds reminders of happy times with your former spouse. Sights, familiar smells, and comfortable fabrics surround you (and your children) with a sense of peace and security. Being in a place filled with happy memories might provide comfort for your grief. For others, the physical surroundings are a constant reminder of pain. Whether it is watching the slow deterioration of a loved one under hospice care or the shock of sudden death, those familiar surroundings may serve as ongoing irritants that chafe against your healing.

One of the wisest pieces of advice I have ever heard is this—Don't make any major decisions for a year. You avoid making knee-jerk reactions you'll later regret.

Don't make any major decisions for a year. You avoid making knee-jerk reactions you'll later regret.

Granted, for some, waiting is not an option. Perhaps financial pressures force an immediate move. For those serving in ministry or in the military, housing is often part of the compensation package, and death results in an immediate move for the survivors.

Moving affects your children, too, even if they are already out of the nest. When a child has lost a parent, having the safety and familiarity of home can be important to their healing. A change in schools and the loss of nearby friends can be particularly turbulent for children still at home. Leaving a safe and familiar home is not easy, no matter the age.

If you eventually feel that moving to a new location is your best or only option, here are a few practical suggestions:

• Get help with the purging process. Trying to go through personal belongings alone is too hard and too emotional. Hiring a professional organizer can help immeasurably. If that's more than you can afford, ask a highly organized friend to help you.

- Remember that getting rid of unwanted belongings is ultimately a gift to your children. Whether you move or stay, it's a painful but important task.

- If you plan to move, decide what things you'll be taking and then hire someone to have a downsizing sale to dispose of the rest.

- Honor your children by allowing them to select some of your husband's personal items after you've done the same. Then, donate the remaining clothes and belongings to a worthwhile charity. Why keep unused garments in boxes when they could help someone in need?

- If possible, consider renting in your new location for a period of time. Make sure it's a place you'll want to live long-term. As a homeowner, you have expenses and hassles and responsibilities of repairs. A lot of freedom comes with renting!

When it feels as though the foundations of your life are shaking due to the loss of your spouse, it's natural to cling to one's physical home as someplace safe and comforting. And yes, I loved the shelter and peace of my home. But, like me, your physical home might eventually need to change as a result of your life's circumstances. I began to pray for the family that would buy our home of thirty years. I wanted them to love it as much as we had and enjoy raising their family there, too.

And, wow, did God answer that prayer! An offer came within two weeks of placing our home on the market. With it came a letter from the wife saying she recognized my name from the seller's disclosure and realized she had been in one of my *Leave Nothing Unsaid* workshops at a local church several years before. She talked about the impact my message had on her and her husband and, as a result, how they had begun keeping journals for their two young children. She shared how much they would love to raise their family in our home. The sweetness of that answered prayer brought a torrent of grateful tears on my part. This precious young couple even brought me a beautiful bouquet of flowers to the closing. God truly did "immeasurably more than I could ask or imagine." (Ephesians 3:20) Although it was still very difficult to leave a home that I loved, that answered prayer made it much easier.

"My people will live in peaceful dwelling places, in secure homes, in undisturbed places of rest."
Isaiah 32:18

CHAPTER ELEVEN

LIVING IN THE PAST

*"Of course you can stay all you want,
it will only cost you your present."*

STOP AND THINK FOR a minute. How much time do you spend every day focusing on the past?

When a season of our life has permanently ended due to the death of our spouse, it's easy to keep staring in the rear-view mirror. We might spend an inordinate amount of time longing for what used to be, wishing our spouse would come back to life. We fantasize about do-overs, wishing for things we could say or take back, longing for one more talk, one more trip, one more embrace, one more dinner together.

We all long for happy endings and our current life circumstances are anything but. That's when we think and rethink about what has happened, somehow hoping that we can think ourselves into a different reality.

A car can't be driven effectively, or safely, if we constantly stare in the rear-view mirror. And we can't move our life forward if we're only focused on the past. As legendary football coach Lou Holtz said: *"The Lord put eyes in front of our head rather than back so we can see where we are going rather than where we have been."*

But what can we do?

First, be aware. It's easy to unconsciously slip into fixating on the past. Paying attention to our thought life is the first step.

Secondly, pray and ask God to show you what's beneficial. Cherish the positive memories. Learn from the past. Honor your late spouse. But move forward. Ask God for fresh dreams and goals for your life. Psalm 37:4 advises: *"Delight yourself in the LORD, and He will give you the desires of your heart."* Those verses don't mean that God is a celestial vending machine. They mean that when we focus on Him, worship Him, and delight in Him, He will place new desires and dreams in our heart.

> *We can't move our life forward if we're only focused on the past.*

Third, focus on the Source of Hope. And sometimes, you simply need to go to bed early! The future always seems to look brighter in the morning. Making a cup of herbal tea, climbing in bed early, simply saying "Jesus, I need you" and reading my Bible has helped me on countless lonely nights.

You really do have control over your thought life. Choose to focus on the good, the hopeful, and the positive things in your life. Make a conscious decision, daily, to worship God, and live in His presence in the present. Be a victor, not a victim!

"Forget the former things; do not dwell on the past.
See, I am doing a new thing!
Now it springs up; do you not perceive it? I am making
a way in the wilderness and streams in the wasteland."
Isaiah 43:18-20

CHAPTER TWELVE

NOTHING WILL REALLY NUMB YOUR PAIN

"This is so much cheaper than therapy!"

GRIEF IS ONE OF the most complicated processes we will ever experience. There's not a ten-step program for quickly navigating through grief. There's no magic formula. There's not a one-size-fits-all, right way and wrong way to grieve. Nor is there an acceptable timetable. Grief is as individual and personal as your fingerprints. Don't let anyone tell you otherwise.

You will experience grief when your spouse dies whether you had the world's greatest marriage or the most difficult. Grief is different for all of us, and the pain is often made more complex as a result of previous losses.

Grief results when our hopes, plans, and dreams do not come true. We lose our best friend and miss them daily. We have sadness because our hopes for that relationship will never be realized. We lose our most trusted confidante and have no one to truly share our joys and sorrows. We miss laughing together, enjoying our children and grandchildren together, traveling together and dreaming about the future together.

Marriage is the most intimate of relationships and was designed to be reflective of Christ and His relationship with the church. We're told that when a couple marries, the two become "one flesh."(Genesis 2:24) Naturally, when a marriage ends for whatever reason, a ripping of that "one flesh" occurs. The relationship is torn apart. Grief is a natural result and healing takes time.

Grief is unpredictable. It hits like waves, often when you least expect it. Grief comes in cycles. The strangest things might trigger your grief: a smell, a song, a meal. At times, you will actually feel physical pain from your grief. The weight of grief is something you seem to carry constantly.

It is natural to want the pain to stop, and it is human nature to grasp at anything within reach to numb the pain. Perhaps it's shopping, shopping and more shopping to buy things you don't need and can't afford. Enough stuff will cause the pain to go away, won't it? No, it will just make your house more cluttered and your bills increase.

Many of us try to use food as a way to numb our pain.

(Our mothers did that for us, didn't they?) One more bowl of ice cream or piece of chocolate will do the trick! Until it doesn't and our clothes don't fit, either.

What about another glass of wine to put you into an alcohol-induced haze? Though you might fall asleep quickly, you'll probably wake up just a few hours later, unable to return to sleep. Combined with the sugar content in wine and likely weight gain, there's also the very real risk of becoming an alcoholic. Don't complicate your problems!

Yes, it's completely understandable to want our pain to cease. But no matter how hard we try and how desperately we grab for relief, we can't change the reality of what has happened.

> *No matter how hard we try and how desperately we grab for relief, we can't change the reality of what has happened.*

As counterintuitive as this might sound, the best way to deal with the grief and associated pain from the loss of a marriage relationship is to *allow yourself to experience the pain*. Don't numb it or deny it. Push through it. Talk about it with those you trust. And constantly cry out to Jesus for His comfort, peace and love. He truly does "*bind up the brokenhearted*." (Psalm 147:3)

The pain of grief will not kill you. It does lessen with time, and your suffering will not be wasted. Someday, God will answer your "why" questions. Maybe that will happen on this side of Heaven. Or, maybe you won't fully understand until you are in Heaven. In the meantime, choose to trust Him with your life—your todays and your tomorrows. Trust Him with the process.

"Blessed are those who mourn,
for they will be comforted."
Matthew 5:4

CHAPTER THIRTEEN

THE SUDDENLY
SINGLE JUNGLE

*"We have so much in common,
and he says he's vegan!"*

"*I WILL NEVER TRY* online dating. *Ever.*" That's what I vehemently and repeatedly proclaimed for years. Until, eventually, I did. And wow, did I live to regret that decision. It wasn't the idea of meeting someone online that was the problem. It was my lack of discernment.

As a result of my experience, do I now warn everyone to avoid online dating sites altogether? No, not at all. 40% of couples who marry today have met online. My advice is to **be very careful**, especially when matched with someone from another geographic location. If you're a trusting soul, you'll naturally tend to believe someone's history. And when you're from different geographic locations, you can't easily verify a person's professional or personal reputation.

When you've been single for a while, it's natural to be lonely. Friday and Saturday nights can be R-E-A-L-L-Y, R-E-A-L-L-Y quiet. You may long for male companionship for dinner and an evening out. Perhaps you've gone weeks or months without even being hugged by another person. You may also be financially blessed as a result of your previously married life. All of that combines to make you a perfect target for the unscrupulous grifter. Please, guard your heart!

When an admirer is charming and chivalrous, it can be easy to believe his promises. And when the banner over his commitment is a professed allegiance to Jesus Christ, it's especially easy to trust him and say yes. Please move slowly and continue to assess whether the "words and music of his life" are in alignment.

No new relationship is worth a broken relationship with your own flesh and blood.

How do your children react to your suitor? My daughter was the only one amongst my many discerning friends who was openly distrustful of my "Prince Charming." I dismissed her concerns as being based on jealousy that someone was diverting my time and attention. And I hurt her deeply by disregarding her reservations. In the end, she was 100% right. I suffered significantly, as did my daughter and all of those who cared about me. Please, listen to your children. Weigh and evaluate their concerns. No new relationship is worth a broken relationship with your own flesh and blood.

Some important things to evaluate as you consider entering into a new, serious relationship:

- How long has he been widowed or divorced? Beware of someone ready to jump too quickly into a new relationship. Grieving the end of a marriage takes time. Clearly, every situation is different, but a man who seems driven to constantly have female companionship might be showing warning signs, especially if his children are still at home and struggling with their own grief.

- Does he have authentic accountability relationships with any other men?

- How has he served the Lord over his lifetime? Have you met people who attest to the impact he has made?

- Is he a spiritual leader? How does he influence you to grow and become more like Jesus?

- Does he respect your moral boundaries, or does he continue to push for premarital intimacy? God's rules don't merely become suggestions based on our age, marital history, or loneliness. Sexual involvement will distort your judgment. Count on it.

- What are his goals, hopes and dreams for the future? What is his attitude about retirement? Does he feel called to continue to serve others in some way? What evidence do you see of that commitment if he is already retired?

- As you begin to seriously discuss marriage, ask to see his last five years of tax returns and be willing to share yours. If you're going to have a truly open and trusting relationship, that includes finances. You can verify his claims about income earned, donations given, etc.

- What is his level of indebtedness? Would he be willing to show you a credit report or credit score? Secrecy or defensiveness about questions like this are red flags for concern.

- Is a sincere, consistent effort shown in developing a relationship with your children?

- What is his relationship like with his own children? Ask them what they love and respect most about their father. Really listen to their answers.

- Is he supportive of your time spent with your children and close friends?

- Is he open to pre-marital counseling? Many believe that if they've been happily married in the past, that there is no need for this. Not true! Combining lives, traditions, families, etc. is very complicated. Far better to talk through the hard issues before getting married than after.

- What about finances? What are his expectations and yours about sharing living expenses? How will you protect your respective children's inheritances? Will he (or you) insist on a pre-nuptial agreement? Estate planning can also be done to protect your respective descendants. Insistence on a pre-nup might mean that your Romeo has no intention of being committed for the long term and wants to protect himself more than you. Does he seem as concerned about your future financial well-being as his own?

• Are you withholding aspects of his behavior (or yours) from those closest to you? If so, ask yourself why. Are you trying to protect someone's image? Are you deceiving yourself about who he really is? Do you see excesses in areas such as spending, eating, drinking, TV watching, or other forms of self-indulgence?

It's easy for someone to say all the right words. The important question is: does he **live** them?

Yes, there are some wonderful, godly, single men out there. And I sincerely hope that you meet one, if that's your heart's desire! Please be aware that the grass is not always greener. At midlife and beyond, the emotional baggage a person brings into a relationship is often heavier. Far better to go slowly, be discerning, and ask hard questions than to experience the pain that results from making a remarriage mistake. One wise approach is to "date through the seasons" before even beginning to discuss marriage. Time eventually reveals truth.

Take it from someone who ignored many red flags. My hope, and earnest prayer, is that my hard-earned wisdom will help you avoid similar heartbreak.

"Guard your heart above all else,
for it determines the course of your life."
Proverbs 4:23 NLT

CHAPTER FOURTEEN

YOU'RE STRONGER
THAN YOU THINK

"I got dressed today!"

"PROMISE ME YOU'LL ALWAYS REMEMBER: *You are braver than you believe, stronger than you seem, and smarter than you think.*" A sign etched with that encouraging quote from Christopher Robin to Pooh was given to me shortly after my husband's death. I hung those words on my kitchen wall and looked at them a LOT as I pressed through hundreds of "I've never done this before" moments. When I couldn't summon the confidence myself, I somehow gained strength from Christopher Robin.

As you walk this unexpected journey, you might need that reminder from Christopher Robin, too! You'll probably have many moments of feeling overwhelmed and thinking the challenges before you are more than you can possibly handle. Others might have pushed through, but it's too much for you.

Nothing could be further from the truth.

You're right about one thing: by yourself, it IS impossible. You can't do this. But you're not alone. As a Christ follower, you have the same power in you that raised Jesus from the dead. (Romans 8:11) Those aren't just words—they're the truth! And you have people that God has put in your life—people who love you—who truly want to help.

I remember being totally overwhelmed by the complex (and completely undocumented) computer and printer network my technologically adept husband had assembled in our home. After his death, the components began to fail, and two different computer technicians were unable find a solution. In frustration, I expressed my quandary to a family friend. The next day, I received a phone call saying that my friend was sending his computer technician to our home to help me. What a godsend and an incredibly thoughtful and generous gesture! If I hadn't expressed my need for help, I would have continued swirling in a technology eddy.

In the midst of my turmoil, my then-teenaged daughter had the wonderful idea to write EVERYTHING that needed to be done on a huge white board which hung in our kitchen.

Getting the tasks out of my ever-muddled brain and written in a visible place was a relief somehow. And then, slowly but surely, I erased each item as it was completed. There was great satisfaction in seeing that once-overwhelming list shrink and finally disappear.

When you're feeling frozen, like a deer caught in the headlights, what should you do?

• Find a verse of Scripture that can be your mantra for strength and encouragement. Repeat it over and over again.

• Pray. Continue to ask God for strength, wisdom and direction. Ask others to pray that for you, too, and don't be shy about being specific.

• Remember that the Holy Spirit and Jesus are interceding for you, too. Really think about that truth. Talk about empowering! (Romans 8:26-27, Hebrews 7:25)

• Ask for help.

• Accept help.

• When you don't know what to do, consult a trusted advisor. You are not on an island and you don't have to figure everything out on your own. Don't feel like you need to be Super Woman.

• Get outside. Take a walk. Breathe. Sometimes, just getting some fresh air and exercise can make a world of difference.

• Make an exhaustive list of **everything** you need to do. Scratch things off, one by one, as you accomplish them. Keep the list so that you can see your progress over time.

- Remember the old adage: "Life by the inch is a cinch. Life by the yard is hard." Take one baby step and then the next. Before long, you'll be shocked to realize you actually are making progress.

- Don't allow negative self-talk to derail you. If you find yourself stuck in that unhealthy pattern, put a rubber band on your wrist and snap it every time you start hearing those same discouraging messages in your head. That physical reminder will help break your negative thinking pattern.

You are not on an island and you don't have to figure everything out on your own.

- If you are truly feeling emotionally paralyzed, talk to your doctor. You might need a short-term anti-depressant or medication to help you sleep. There's nothing wrong with taking prescribed medication to help you through the valley.

- Utilize Christian counseling resources for practical support. Consult your church, the Association of Christian Counselors (AACC.net), or trusted friends for recommendations.

- Keep a notebook by your bed and each night, write down two or three things you accomplished that day. Maybe it's only "I got out of bed today." But that's something!

- Celebrate the small victories. Don't focus on all that looms ahead. Be grateful for every step of progress.

One of the greatest things I've learned over the last decade is to press on. Again, and again, I've seen that *"My God will* meet all your needs according to the riches of His glory in Christ Jesus." (Philippians 4:19) Countless times, I've whispered: "*I can't do this.*" And that still, small voice inside of me reminds me: "*You're absolutely right. But I can. And I AM.*"

"But those who trust in the Lord will find new strength.
They will soar high on wings like eagles. They will run
and not grow weary. They will walk and not faint."
Isaiah 40:31 NLT

CHAPTER FIFTEEN

AN ATTITUDE OF GRATITUDE

*"She's had a hard time finding a job since her human
started counting blessings instead."*

DO YOU EVER EMBARRASS YOURSELF? I certainly do.
And what embarrasses me the most is when I find myself
grumbling and complaining about what I **don't** have instead
of being incredibly grateful for all of my blessings.

President Theodore Roosevelt once astutely observed
that *"comparison is the thief of joy."* Most of us only compare
ourselves to those who have more, better, or something we
want. When that's our focus, we're anything but joyful.

When the hot water in the shower runs out, we don't

think about the child in Africa walking miles to fill up a jug of clean water. We complain about not getting a close parking spot, forgetting about our wheelchair-bound friend who would give anything to take just one step. We grumble that "we're starving" when we've had our last meal just a few hours ago.

And when our spouse has died, our natural response is to feel sorry for ourselves and bemoan our situation. Yes, it is extremely healthy to express our grief and sorrow when we have experienced great loss. There will come a time when you will begin to see God's blessings, again, too.

You can't hold two thoughts in your mind at the same time. If you are focusing on daily reasons for gratitude, you won't be able to be spend as much time reciting every verse of "Woe is Me." Perhaps it is receiving a loving and unexpected text message from a friend. Or seeing a beautiful sunrise. Enjoying the wonderful aroma of fresh basil. When you become a noticer and look for the countless ways God is blessing you, you'll be amazed at all the reasons you have on a daily basis to say, "thank you, Lord."

Become a private detective and search for four or five reasons to be grateful each day.

One of the best disciplines you can develop is the habit of keeping a daily gratitude journal. Become a private detective and search for four or five reasons to be grateful each day. Write them down. Do it again tomorrow. This practice won't bring your spouse back, but you will find your attitude improving. As days turn into weeks and months, you will be able to look back and see God's faithfulness to you and His love for you in ways that will fill you with joy. Your anthem will become "Great Is Thy Faithfulness."

"Summing it all up, friends, I'd say you'll do best by filling your minds and meditating on things true, noble, reputable, authentic, compelling, gracious – the best, not the worst; the beautiful, not the ugly; things to praise, not things to curse."
Philippians 4:8 The Message

CHAPTER SIXTEEN

THE SUN WILL COME UP IN THE MOURNING

"So you CAN teach an old dog new tricks!"

DO ME A FAVOR. Go, grab a hand mirror. Hold it right in front of your mouth for a minute. Did it fog up? Congratulations! You're still breathing! And if you're still breathing, God has purpose and meaning for your life!

It's natural when a loved one dies or when a marriage ends to conclude that God is finished with us. Nothing could be further from the truth. We could wrongly assume that if our role as wife is over, we don't have anything left to contribute. We might shift our entire focus to be the world's best grandmother. That's wonderful, if you are so blessed. But as part of the body of Christ (1 Corinthians 12), we are called to do more than just love our own children and grandchildren.

No, you're not too old. I know you're tired; probably bone weary from grief. But one of the greatest things you can do to breathe life back into your broken heart is to serve others.

Think about the parable of the talents in Matthew 25. Even if you don't feel you have much to offer, please don't "bury" your talents. Ask God how He wants you to serve Him. Start small. Maybe it's volunteering somewhere once a week. Making a meal for a friend going through a hard time. Buying flowers for someone who is lonely. Signing up for a mission trip. Helping others who are hurting will bless and encourage you, I promise. Consider it a love offering for God.

When we turn the focus off of ourselves, our circumstances, and begin to help and comfort others, our attitude naturally improves. As you grieve and adjust to life without your partner, you are in a new season of learning and discovery. Experiment with different ways of serving. Step outside of your comfort zone. I know it's not easy. God will give you the grace to do it. And you will be truly amazed at how you will grow and how God will use you to bless others' lives!

"For we are God's handiwork, created in Christ Jesus to do good works, which God prepared in advance for us to do."
Ephesians 2:10

CHAPTER SEVENTEEN

THE ONLY GUY WHO WILL NEVER LEAVE YOU

*"Jesus, I know you're with me,
but I could really use a hug."*

NIGHT AFTER NIGHT, YOU'RE reminded that your life has changed forever. The pillow next to yours is empty. There are no arms to hold you. Your life partner is gone forever.

In those times of searing heartache, it is easy to feel completely and totally alone, as though you're adrift at sea or marooned on a desert island. And in those dark times, it's vitally important that you counteract your feelings with facts.

You might feel alone, but you are not alone. As a Christ follower, you can cling to the truth that Jesus is with you.

His promise was recorded in Matthew 28:20: *"I am with you always, to the very end of the age."*

And if you know about Jesus, but don't really know Him personally, now is the perfect time to meet Him and fall in love. The Gospel truly is the world's best love story.

Why?

• Jesus promises to never leave you or forsake you. (Hebrews 13:5-6)

• You can trust Him completely. Jesus will never betray you nor let you go. (John 10:28)

• Jesus doesn't condemn you for anything you've ever done or not done. (Romans 8:1, John 8:11)

• He offers you complete forgiveness for every mistake, sin and hurtful thought and action. How? All Jesus asks is that you admit you have missed the mark and ask Him to forgive you for your sins. Ask Jesus to be your Lord and Savior. He died to take the punishment for your sins. Surrendering your life to Jesus is the best, wisest, most rewarding decision you will ever make. (John 3:15-16, John 10:15, John 11:25-26)

• He is praying for you. (Romans 8:34)

• He is already preparing a home for you in Heaven. How wonderful is that? (John 14:2)

• Jesus sent the Comforter, the Holy Spirit, to live with you forever. (John 14:16-17)

• He offers you peace. He doesn't want you to be troubled or afraid. (John 14:27)

• Despite the loss you have experienced, Jesus wants you

to have a full and abundant life in the days ahead. (John 10:10)

• He will give you the strength you need. (Philippians 4:13) You don't have to do it on your own.

• He will supply all of your needs. (Philippians 4:19)

• Jesus will enable you to be fruitful with your life. (John 15:5)

• Jesus offers you true rest for your soul. (Matthew 11:28-29)

Ask Jesus to be your Lord and Savior. Cry out to Him in your times of loneliness. No, you won't see Him physically, but He will be with you in Spirit. He will comfort and encourage you. He will bind up your broken heart and restore your hope. He loves you more deeply and perfectly than you can fully grasp or imagine, and He always will.

Listening to worship music has helped fill my home and my mind with truth. I've found that the best nightcap is reading or listening to one of the Gospels and thinking about Jesus as I drift off to sleep. On especially sleepless nights, I'll go through the alphabet from A to Z, praising God for an attribute that corresponds with each letter. I will review my gratitude journal and reflect on the countless ways God has provided for me. I remember that I am perfectly, securely, and completely loved. Always and forever.

Jesus is with you, always. And that's the best life partner you could ever have!

Whether your spouse has died, or your marriage ended

for other reasons, you are in a new and unexpected state of singleness at this season of life. Please continue to remind yourself that single does not equal alone. Jesus is with you, always. And that's the best life partner you could ever have!

"May your roots go down deep into the soil of God's marvelous love. And may you have the power to understand, as all God's people should, how wide, how long, how high, and how deep His love really is. May you experience the love of Christ, though it is so great that you will never fully understand it. Then you will be filled with the fullness of life and power that comes from God."
Ephesians 3:17-20 NLT

CHAPTER EIGHTEEN

MY PRAYERS FOR YOU

"Hey, I wrote this new song just for you.
Are you ready?"

Dear Friend,

Thank you so much for reading my book. For many years, I've wanted to share these truths with other women who are hurting. I hope it's been helpful. Please know that I am praying for you as you walk this difficult journey.

I am praying that God will bind up your broken heart and give you fresh, green hope for the future.

I am praying that He will put a new song in your mouth and new dreams in your heart.

I am praying that, eventually, you will want to comfort others with the comfort that you have received.

I am praying that you will be an example to friends and family of what's possible when life doesn't go as planned.

And I am praying that God will give you the gift of laughter amidst your tears.

I'd love to hear from you. You can contact me at *www. JodyNoland.com.*

In His Love,

Jody

"He has given me a new song to sing, a hymn of praise
to our God. Many will see what He has done and
be astounded. They will put their trust in the Lord."
Psalm 40:3 NLT

WITH GRATITUDE

FIRST AND FOREMOST, thank you to The Faithful One, my Lord and Savior, Jesus Christ. Thank you for Your unconditional, redemptive love for me and for the countless ways You continue to bless me. I pray that You will use this book and the lessons You have taught me to bless and encourage others and to draw readers to Yourself.

My deepest gratitude to all of my dear friends who comprise the Leave Nothing Unsaid Prayer Team. This special group of people have been interceding for me and my calling for many years, including praying for my work on this book. Y'all have truly been the "wind beneath my wings."

I am so thankful for the faithful friends who spent so much time reading and providing thoughtful input on this book. Heartfelt thanks to Kelly Brewer, Penny Crump,

Beverly Elliott, Valerie Michels, Terry Noel, Anne Noland, Susan Ohly, Joy Seidner and Lexi Wayman.

Thank you to Dr. Bill Byrd, Joy Seidner, Ann Sherin and Debby Temmer. Each of you has been so helpful to me in my long and winding journey of growth. God has used your wisdom and encouragement to help me sort out my jumbled emotions, learn from my painful life experiences and "smile at the days to come." I am profoundly grateful.

My deepest gratitude to Bryan Jordin for his unendingly generous support for my work with Leave Nothing Unsaid and Good Grief! and for his encouragement to press on with my calling despite the challenging headwinds of life.

And, finally, thank **you** for reading! I pray that you found help, hope and even a little humor in these pages.

If you'd like to receive a weekly dose of encouragement (my blog), please sign up on *www.JodyNoland.com*.

---

*"The Lord bless you and keep you; the Lord make His face
to shine upon you and be gracious to you; the Lord lift his
countenance upon you and give you peace."*
Numbers 6:24-26

ABOUT THE AUTHOR

JODY NOLAND'S MISSION is to encourage people and to inspire others to do the same. As founder and CEO (Chief Encouragement Officer) of the Leave Nothing Unsaid movement, she has spent the last decade equipping people around the world to practice authentic, lasting affirmation to those who matter most. From her own lived experience, her writing is founded on the belief that we can always find purpose in our struggles and that we can always find reasons to laugh. Connect with her at *www.JodyNoland.com*.

If this book was helpful to you, please leave an Amazon review and give copies to others who might benefit. Many thanks!

Photograph of the author by Meshali Mitchell.